CW00346543

This is Just What it's Like Sometimes

Messages of Healing, Hope + Reclamation

Neghar Fonooni

All words by Neghar Fonooni
Book design by Aimée Suen
Author photo by Homer Parkes

Alchemized in Los Angeles. Printed in the United States.
Find out more at saltandsorcery.shop

For the hearts that stay open when they're broken, when they're raw.

For the hands that wield magic, from the cosmos, from within.

For anyone who needs to exhale.

For everyone who wants to come home.

Contents

And so it is
(a preface)

I loved someone and he left. It's not as simple as that, but it's not especially complex, either—a tale as old as time. I know I'm not alone in the sticky mess of my mangled heart. I know that pain is universal, that you've been there, too.

In the interest of healing I did what I've always done, the only thing I know how to do when nothing makes sense. I wrote, and as each word took shape, I found lost pieces of myself, reclaimed them, reconditioned them, brought them to the foreground of my being.

What follows are a handful of essays written during the dark night of my soul. They talk about healing— about grief and hope, the transmutation of our pain into some kind of spiritual, creative gold. They're the messages I channeled when my wounds were raw and the only balm that seemed to calm them was the *tap tap tap* of my keyboard.

It was helpful to me, as I crawled through the abyss, to remember that *this is just what it's like sometimes*. It won't be like this all the time.

There's magic in the shadows, and afterwards, when

the shadows have done what they came to do, there is something else entirely.

In between it all there can be joy, even in the grief, even in the darkness, even as we are altogether rent asunder. Nothing lasts forever, not this poison nor this portal—not the promises or the pain of them unkept.

I cried into my pillow and into the void. I reached out into the cosmos for something to keep me tethered and these words were what it gave me. And now, I offer them to you.

I hope you find some solace in these words. I hope they help you breathe when breathing feels like the most impossible thing. I hope they remind you of the magic in your bones.

Most of all, I hope that when it's *just like that sometimes*, you'll know it's like that for me, too. For the Collective. For so many other fractured hearts and languid travelers, for everyone out there just trying to find their way home.

They don't need to be read in the order they're presented here. Close your eyes, make a wish, ask the Universe to flip the pages. Where you land is where you're meant to be.

And so it is.

With Love + Salt,

Neghar

Grieve

I've cried on most of the last 180 days.

I've cried myself to sleep, cried in the kitchen making coffee, in the closet staring at empty hangers, in the middle of the night when I realize I'm alone—and it wasn't just a dream.

I've cried at the gym, in the shower, in my parked car, twice on an airplane, and once at the grocery store when I realized I had too much food in my cart for just one person.

I've cried with people who love me, people who are filled to the brim with rage on my behalf, people who would walk to the ends of the earth to keep my tears from falling. And I've cried in front of strangers, too.

Because this is just what it's like sometimes.

It's raw and ragged and sharp around the edges. Life doesn't usually go according to plan—stories have plot twists and surprise endings. People get hurt.

People leave. People change their minds. *Forever* and *always* don't mean what we think they mean.

There are moments when all we can feel is the deep gash of unkept promises.

I hope in those moments you know how absolutely not alone you are, despite the temptation to feel otherwise. Pain is not a unique experience and heartbreak isn't foreign to most of us. We've all felt the sting of betrayal, the sudden burst of a bubble, the tragedy of a bitter end.

We all know how it feels to cry into a pillow, to scream into the night, to shake our fists at the sky and curse the gods. We've all inhabited our own universe of grief, at one time or another.

And I'd like to think, on some level, in some small way, that it's part of what connects us—part of what weaves its way through our shared experience of being human. Our shared pain. Our collective broken hearts that refuse to stop beating.

I'd like to think that through my tears I can send a ripple of something out into the world, something soft and quiet, something with the capacity to heal.

I'd like to think—to hope—that in reading my words, in hearing me recount the raw experience of my pain, you see some of yourself reflected back at you, and know, with utmost certainty, that we are all the children of these bright and burning stars.

That we are altogether howling at the moon.

Cling

Everything dies, in its own time, in its own way. Everything must go—

Nothing gold can stay.

Leaves will turn and fall and crumple beneath our feet. Suns will rise only to set once more, dipping below the horizon, laying one more day to rest, another rotation of this rock we call home.

Love comes and love goes. Hearts heal and hearts break, only to heal again. Little babies grow into their fullness. Things don't always go as planned. Something we thought was forever suddenly ceases to exist at all.

And still, we *cling*.

We cling so tightly, so desperately. We hold on to things even as they beg to be let go—because of comfort, because of familiarity, because of fear.

We fear the unknown, the uncertain, the unresolved.

Most of all, we fear having to face that things didn't

turn out the way they were *supposed* to. We stay longer than we should, because we *can't stand* the idea that we couldn't make it work. We hold on so tightly—to grudges, to cold hands and dead hearts, to love that no longer loves us back.

We keep things past their expiration date, keep them in our pockets, our hearts, our mouths. And in doing so, we suffer. We suffer *so* much.

The tree doesn't fight the loss of its leaves. It mourns them, perhaps. It laments. It grieves. But ultimately, it allows dead things to die. It knows that as they fall, the branches are made ready for new growth, when the time is right and the winds are warmer.

We don't *have* to grip as tightly as we do. There are other options—ones that might hurt, at least initially, but will heal us entirely.

We *can* let dead things die and decompose. We can throw them into the fire, watch them burn into ash. We can offer those ashes back to the earth, dig graves to dance upon until the land is fertile once again— until our hands feel ready to plant something new.

We don't *have* to cling.

We can weep and mourn and yearn for time to move in reverse, all while knowing it's time to put nail to coffin, all while accepting it's time to move on.

And when we do, we'll know what it is to breathe again—to let dead things die and make space for the living, to close one loop as we open another.

Crumbs

Autumn has been my therapist for the past several years. She guided me through the ashes of my divorce, watched me fall in love again, and welcomed me back with open arms when that love turned to ashes, too.

She's the one who taught me about crumbs.

I learned in my twenties, when I started my spiritual exploration, that I have a tendency to give too much—to give far more than I receive. I learned about co-dependent relationships and the role I played in them.

I learned, most of all, that healers and empaths are susceptible to this type of giving, the kind that doesn't offer room for receiving. I worked to create that space, to fill it with worthiness.

But I didn't learn about crumbs.

I didn't yet know, on a conscious level, that I was often willing to receive the bare minimum of affection, attention, and adoration from a lover.

That I was content to just be chosen, even if being chosen meant feeling lonely in my relationships. That I didn't ask to receive the love I deserved and desired, because I was too afraid asking would lead to fighting, and fighting would lead to leaving.

I habitually subsisted on crumbs.

In every single romantic relationship I've been in, I've subsisted on crumbs, and I've been close to starving.

And it's not because I don't believe I'm worthy, because trust me, I do. I like myself and love myself and am, without hyperbole, my own biggest fan. I know I'm worthy of the same levels of love and respect that I dole out, yet I have often found myself accepting otherwise.

Out of fear.

Out of scarcity.

Out of comfort.

So when Autumn pointed out that I'd been on a *crumb diet*—that I'd allowed myself to subsist on morsels and scraps—it was like swallowing a truth serum and trying to cough it up.

"But they're such delicious crumbs!" I argued. "Crumbs are better than nothing at all!" I protested.

And of course, I *knew* I was fooling myself. I knew she was right. And also of course, I kept accepting the crumbs, despite knowing better. In fact, I went on to accept *new* crumbs, from a new plate, in a new relationship, with a new man.

Until the day I mustered up the courage to ask for a whole meal, and that man left me faster than he could turn on the damn stove.

The part I'd feared about leaving was true. But the part I knew about *deserving* was truer.

I knew—I know—I deserve the whole damn meal. Five courses. Wine pairings. Two options for dessert—because maybe I want something chocolatey, and maybe I don't. I know I deserve that meal from a partner just as much I deserve it from myself.

I found myself nourished in his absence.

I cried and healed and screamed and grieved, that much is true. But I filled my plate, too. I chose, once and for all, to get off the crumb diet, and only sit at tables of abundance and reciprocity.

I allowed the Universe to nourish me, to pour blessings into my cup, even if those blessings felt like curses, even if it meant saying goodbye.

I made promises to myself, to my heart and my hunger, to say no to anything that offered me less than I deserved. I'm keeping those promises.

I promise that much.

Soft

Sometimes the hardest thing to do is stay soft.

Sometimes, when things are hard, your heart will choose to harden too. You'll clench your jaw and ball your fists and curse the gods with bitter tongue.

Life will sucker punch you—because that's just what life does—and as you're doubled over in pain, the dark side will seduce you. It will tempt you toward the jagged edges of apathy. It will ask that you harden the parts of you that are meant to love and trust and hope and wish.

It's easier to become jaded than it is to *not*.

When nothing goes as planned, when your heart is broken and your bones are aching and your lashes are soaked in salt—choosing to be cynical feels almost *liberating*.

If you're hard, you can't be hurt. If you're hopeless, you can't be hoodwinked. If you don't think anything will go your way, you won't be disappointed when it doesn't—because oftentimes, it won't.

Maybe the Universe has told you one too many cosmic jokes, and it's not so funny anymore. Maybe you're over it. Maybe enough is enough. It's easier to give in, to let the storm take you.

But maybe, despite all of that, you'll remain *soft around the edges*, hopeful at the seams. Maybe you'll choose to believe that hearts have an *infinite* capacity to heal—to grow more radiant, more supple, more full.

Maybe you'll grow in the ways that one can only grow when they pick up the heavy things and explore the weight of them with curiosity and trust.

Because the heavy things will never cease. The storms will keep coming. The maelstroms will persist.

And so will you.

That's not to say you won't get a little salty along the way, and that's okay, too. There can be salt and shadows and ruckus and rage, but alongside them hope *must* reside. Hope is the most important thing of all.

Hope will keep you soft, when life gets hard. Hope will keep you grounded, when the walls around you crumble. Hope must stay sewn into the edges of your heart, for rainy days, for rescue.

Okay

"It's going to be okay." I said it out loud.

I speak to myself mostly out loud these days—maybe it's age, maybe it's some sort of evolution. Maybe it's just how I've learned to communicate with myself, by myself. I like it, speaking to myself out loud. It feels more real that way, less margin for error.

"It's going to be okay," I reassured myself while crying in the shower.

And then:

"I mean, it's going to *suck*. But it's also going to be okay."

I've cried in the shower so many times. I know you have, too. It just *feels* like the right place to cry. There aren't any *wrong* places to bare your soul, but there are some that just feel *more* right.

In the shower.

Into a pillow.

Out in the great wide open, under a canopy of stars, swaddled by the light of the moon.

This was my first shower in days. I'd spent a week in the same sweatpants, barely eating, finding it difficult to exist. When something shatters—when something shifts in undesired, unexpected ways—there's often a period of shock that follows.

This was mine.

As the first week stretched into the second, and the shock turned to genuine sadness, I managed to activate enough energy to get into the shower. To cleanse, as a double entendre of sorts. To weep. To begin again, the process of healing.

But this wasn't the kind of shower where I slumped to the depths of the tile beneath my feet, to sob in a nearly fetal position. I leaned against the shower wall, broken open but refusing to fall apart—somehow a mess and a miracle, simultaneously, in turns.

I am a woman who has spent years in deep reflection and extensive shadow work—not always by choice, but purposefully, nonetheless.

I have walked with demons that were mine and many that were not. I have made the same mistake as many times as I needed to in order to finally break the spell. I have unpacked and unraveled and unlearned in search of my own alignment, of the alchemy of my soul.

I have cried in the shower before and I will do so again.

So, with encouraging sobs and tears spiked with courage, I consoled myself: *You're going to hurt, for a long while, most likely. You're going to cry in this shower again, and in other places too. And then, when the work is done, you'll be okay. But not yet.*

I wasn't in a hurry to be okay. Like I said, I've done this demon dance before. I know that healing exists on its own timeline, and that timeline is anything but linear. I know that shadow work and heartbreak and cord cutting are the suckiest things...until they're not.

I know that it's okay not to be okay.

It's okay to cry in the shower, on a park bench, in the cereal aisle of the grocery store. It's okay to still be healing, to heal again, to do that in a spiral. It's okay to know you're going to be okay even as you suffer, even as you grieve. You have to do that for awhile.

You have to do that for as long as it takes.

Heal

Being alive means that you will *hurt*.

To live is to feel deeply, and much of that feeling is made up of pain. Not all of it, of course. There is joy, too—sometimes concurrently. But for now we'll focus on pain, because we're exploring what it means to heal. Hurt and heal are two sides of the same coin, and that coin is, well, *life*.

Being alive also means that you will *heal*.

You will break into pieces without falling apart. You will put the shattered fragments of yourself back together in some new and miraculous way. You will hold your breath and breathe again, because you went through something and came out the other side.

Being alive is doing that, over and over.

Exposing the tender flesh of your heart to uncertain elements, tending to its wounds and honoring its scars, again and again. It sounds redundant—pointless even—when distilled down so simply. But if we do it consciously—the healing part—it's *alchemy*.

It's why we're here.

Every hurtful ordeal, every shadow, every struggle becomes a healing opportunity that *expands* us, evolves us, brings us closer to our center.

If we never hurt, we will never heal. And if we never heal—if we don't know what it's like to travel the dark night of the soul, if we never learn to cast a Patronus charm—we won't truly know the depths of ourselves, the width of our magic.

But we can only do this—the hurting, the healing, subsequently, in a spiral—if we *feel* the pain without *becoming* the pain. We can't let the sadness become stagnant within us; the pain is not a resident, it's merely a visitor, passing through.

We've *got* to feel it, *all* of it, that much is true. That much is necessary. But it has to flow through. It has to keep moving. It cannot become cellular. It cannot burrow into your bones.

You have to flip the coin.

Because even as you are *hurting*—even as your heart aches and your tears run and you feel your wounds ooze and your scars itch—you are *not* those things. You are not your pain. You are not your suffering.

Even as you trudge through the swamps of sadness, you are not a sad *person*. You are a person feeling sadness. And even still, you are a celestial creature, having a *human experience* of sadness.

You are stardust.

You were born to heal. To witness and honor and process your pain.

To break the cycle of trauma in your bloodline.

To bring the Divine into your lineage.

You were never meant to let the pain become you.

Tequila

The weekend I celebrated my 37th trip around the sun wasn't the *most* tequila I've drank in that span of time, but it was pretty close. Top five for sure.

It was also the weekend I learned about *joy*—or at least, how I was rejecting it.

We were in Palm Springs, my dearest friends and I, and it had only been a few weeks since he'd left. The day before we drove to the desert, he came to collect the last of his things. I'd been asking him to do so for weeks, but I guess he was too busy with his new life, his new love.

He was supposed to come with us to Palm Springs, originally. Instead, he was loading up a truck with the final shreds of evidence that we'd ever shared a life together.

I stood awkwardly in front of him and said, "I don't know how to be around you anymore." He offered a weak apology and walked away carrying an odd assortment of things: a lamp, a stack of records, my heart.

I watched him until he was out of sight, and I watched even after. He never looked back. I never saw that version of him again, because the next time I saw him, he was a stranger. But that's a story for another day.

I carried the pain of that moment with me to the desert. Despite the tequila and the palm trees and the relentless love and support of my friends, I carried a sadness with me that was so heavy it all but smothered me.

On my back, in the grass, beneath the merciless warmth of the desert summer sun, I sobbed quietly. Discreetly.

This was supposed to be a celebration, and here I was, inhabiting my own universe of grief.

But as I lay there, tear streaked, bereft, feeling the weight of his absence, something within me began to shift. Maybe it was the desert wind, the whispers it carries, subtle messages from the Universe. Every gust of wind is some kind of a spell, some organic invocation; I think you've felt that, too.

Or maybe it was just the tequila.

Either way, a shift ensued. Not from sadness to gladness or even acceptance, but a tiny push in the direction of joy—a reminder that joy can coexist with pain, that heartbreak and lightheartedness are not mutually exclusive.

I heard my friends laughing inside the house and I thought, I can be sad and still laugh with them. I don't need to build an altar for my heartbreak, a shrine to my sadness. I can honor the loss I've experienced—the way that it broke me open—without also rejecting my joy.

I can walk with these shadows without becoming them.

Shadow work doesn't have to be dark, exclusively. There can be light. There can be joy. There can be tequila. They can all coexist. We can celebrate, even as we mourn. We are not meant to worship at the altar of our pain, even as we process, even as we heal.

We can inhabit our very own universe of grief, and there can be joy there. We can give ourselves permission to receive it. This is an act of faith. This is what will carry us through.

Receive

We're never as alone as we think we are.

It's hard not to feel that way, of course. The world is a complicated place with complicated problems; we're all just trying to survive the day, the week, the year. It's hard not to feel alone in this quest for survival, because the truth is, *no one is coming to save us*.

But another truth that's just as real, just as true, just as certain is that *nobody does it alone*.

The only way to survive this world—to thrive in this world—is to realize that none among us are meant to get through it completely on our own. We don't have to do everything with our own two hands. We don't have to wear all the hats and play all the roles. We can share the hats. We can delegate the roles.

We can *lean* on someone.

We can ask.

We can receive.

We can, but we don't always. Asking is hard. Receiving is harder.

Believing that it's safe to ask—okay to ask—that we're worthy of receiving, these are the hardest.

No one is coming to save you, but you don't need to be saved. You only need to be supported, to be held in the womb of the collective, to open your cup and let other people fill it—to allow the blessings to come through.

Because the blessings *will* come through, and when they do, you need to be capable of recognizing them. You need to be ready to receive them.

Burn

The fireplace in my bedroom has never been used to build a fire.

I've burned things in it, but not wood. Not twigs or kindling. Just memories—well, the *evidence* of them, at least.

Because the memories are still mine.

The image of him punching away at his typewriter, crafting the love notes I would later offer to the fire. The way his skin always smelled like Irish Spring. The weight of his body next to me in the middle of the night. The sound of his often maniacal laugh—how it made me want to laugh with him forever.

Those aren't things I can or even want to burn, but I can burn the poems. The notes. Polaroid pictures, drawings, and scribbles. The many scraps of paper I kept in a jar on my altar that told the story of our love.

I offered them to the fire, one after the other, flames

licking carelessly at the words he so carefully penned, all of it turning to ember. To ash. To dust.

With each offering I felt myself exhale just a little more deeply, each page lifting an ounce of weight from my heart as it entered the fire. The first burn was catharsis, but it wasn't the last. As time passed, I continued to find pieces of him pressed between pages, stuck to the bottom of drawers, ghosts that hadn't yet found their way to the grave.

And I offered those to the fire, as well. One by one, piece by piece, breath by breath.

I know that I can't erase him, nor do I want to. What we shared was real, at least for me. It happened. It *changed* me.

But if I want to slither out of this skin and into one that's more fitting for this next chapter of my life—if I want to cut the cords that keep me tethered to the pain of losing, of leaving, of being left—I know that requires an offering. I know there are things I must burn.

To burn is not to forget.

It's not avoidance, denial, or indifference. It isn't an escape or a cop out—it's a ritual.

To burn is to process. To cleanse. To **heal**. To honor the past while choosing to stay fully committed to the present. To "throw roses into the abyss and give thanks to the monsters who didn't succeed in swallowing you alive." [*Nietzsche*]

There are things we will need to throw into the fire—things we must watch burn and blister and turn to ash. There are ashes we must gather and offer to the sea. There are pieces of our past selves, remnants of our past lives, that must be offered to the fire as a message, as a spell.

"I have walked through the fire, and the fire has forged me."

It's through this offering, through the messages we send into the smoke, into the ether, that we are made whole once again.

Phoenix

I wish I could tell you that it's easy to get back up.

That you'll rise without question. That you'll fight without falter. I wish I could tell you that showing up, even when you're shattered, feels like a balm, smooth as Neosporin, clean as a long, hot shower.

But the truth is, getting back up *hurts*.

Sometimes it feels like jagged glass, protruding from open wounds, the sticky drip of your soul laid bare upon the earth. And sometimes it feels like gravity is working overtime, pulling you deeper into the core of this rock, down into the abyss of what was "supposed to be," the void of broken promises.

It isn't easy to rise, when you've fallen, when you're falling. It's the hardest thing, actually. It's much easier to stay down, at the bottom. It's quiet there, in the wreckage, in the wake.

But you do it anyway. You get back up, despite every reason to do otherwise.

Even though it hurts. Even when it's hard, when it's heavy, when it's the very last thing you want to do. You get up, tear streaked face and aching bones. You get up, heart cautiously open, feet planted firmly on the earth. You get up, magic in your muscles, in your veins, at the very tips of your fingers.

Because you are the Maiden, the Mother, the Crone. You are the magic you've been seeking. You are the Phoenix—the one who has died a myriad times, danced on your own grave, eye to eye with Hades, hand in hand with the darkness.

And you know these deaths are not final—you know, at your center, at your core, that from these ashes you must rise. You know—because you've done so before and you will do so again—that every time you rise, you rise higher.

You know that when you pull the jagged glass from your wounds, when you stitch and you sew and you smooth the scars of every gouge and gash, you'll *rise*. Stronger. Wiser. More agile than before.

You know that even though it's hard and it's heavy and it hurts right down to your bones, that it's worth it, too. Even as the flames lick your skin and melt your flesh you have faith in your own reanimation. You know that even as some part of you is dying, the whole of you will be reborn.

Because it's what you were born to do. Again, again, again.

Treasure

"I'm so proud of you," I said to myself in the mirror, shortly after waking.

It had been two months since he'd left me. Since he'd ended our long and loving relationship with a short string of words sent capriciously over text. Since the bed had become too big and the closet half empty. Since my heart and my head began trying—in tandem and apart—to make sense of things that didn't make sense.

The nights were the hardest, but let's be honest, the mornings were hard too. I'd lay in bed and say to myself, "All you have to do is get out of bed, babygirl." Once I got out of bed I'd say, "You *just* have to open the curtains." And then make coffee. And then get dressed. And then and then and then, until it was night again.

On this morning, this day that marked exactly two months of talking myself out of bed and into life, I looked in the mirror and for the first time, I was proud.

I was still mostly raw and partly hollowed out, but I was proud, too.

I stared back at myself, face streaked with tears, curly hair a tangled mess, body cloaked in my favorite robe—the one with the hood and pockets; the one that always feels like home.

My dreams the night before had left me feeling a little more tender around my heart's edges, a little more broken open than when I'd closed my eyes and laid my head to rest.

Underneath it all I was naked—physically, emotionally, energetically—able to see myself fully in a rare, sincere moment when I wasn't trying to convince anyone I was doing okay.

"I'm so proud of you, because you have every reason to stop showing up, and you keep doing so anyway."

This wasn't the first plot twist the Universe had written into my life, but it certainly was the most shocking thus far. It sent me reeling in ways I didn't know I could reel, healing again after years of thinking I'd done all the healing one person could do.

It was an earthquake—unpredictable and devastating; I fumbled around for something solid to keep me from falling, and what I found was myself.

Staring back.

No one sets out on the Fool's Journey seeking resilience. We seek love, connection, belonging, treasure—we seek our dreams, we seek our destiny. Resilience is what we get when things don't go as planned; resilience is the real treasure.

"I am so proud of you," I said. "You have survived every struggle, climbed every hill, slayed every dragon. And you just. Keep. Showing. Up."

Every morning in July and then into August, day after day, I got out of bed. I kept opening the curtains. I kept making the coffee and getting dressed and taking on the day as best I could.

And I kept crying myself to sleep, too. I kept writing poems about broken hearts and broken promises, listening to the same song on repeat, saying the same things over and over to my closest friends as I processed, as I healed.

And I kept standing in front of the mirror, reminding myself what a miracle it was to see my reflection looking back. To be here in this moment, breathing, feeling, almost falling and always rising. To show up and wield the resilience I'd earned—not as a weapon, and not as a shield—as a prize. As a trophy. As a treasure.

Leviosa

A tattoo on the inside of my right forearm reads, "Leviosa" in blackletter font. It's a spell, and as such, a reminder.

All of my tattoos are reminders, of course—talismans of who I've become and who I'm becoming, keepsakes in permanent ink. But this one, the one derived from *Wingardium Leviosa*—the levitation charm introduced in *Harry Potter and the Sorcerer's Stone*— is especially significant.

To a small extent, this tattoo is a cheeky little nod to my longtime love of lifting weights, but that's just the icing. *Leviosa*, at least to me, is about ascension.

We've all been given opportunities for ascension, opportunities that look a lot like curses, curses that are actually *blessings* in disguise.

Sometimes a curse *is* just a curse, but most often it's a blessing, too.

Most often, the Fool, the Seeker, the Heroine in our story is challenged in ways that seem devastating at first, but are expansive in the end. She leaves the comfort of the ordinary world and enters the abyss—not to be broken and defeated—but to be transformed, renewed, resurrected.

Death. Rebirth. Again. Again.

When you travel through the dark night of the soul you are not being punished—you're being *initiated*. Each threshold of this journey is a portal. Every skin you shed, an offering. Each curse, a blessing.

It's the most difficult thing to believe when you're in the thick of it, but it's the truest thing, nonetheless.

When you're in the abyss—when the shadows are dense and demons lurk in every corner—it's hard to see past them, to see the blessings on the other side. It's easiest, of course, to feel resentful. To lament what seems like bad fortune. To see the darkness as a curse.

I won't ask you to be grateful for the darkness, at least not while you're in it. When you're weary and drained and bone tired, the last thing you want is to be told you should be grateful. How patronizing. How trite.

But I will ask you to *believe*.

Believe that you have what it takes to break curses.

Believe that most curses aren't curses at all, but blessings, masquerading.

Believe that you are worthy of these blessings.

Believe that even as you journey the dark night of the soul, there is a purpose for this pain, that your pain is a portal.

Believe, most of all, that you will ascend, as you always have, as you will once more.

Find something—anything—to keep you tethered to this belief, because you'll need it when you enter the abyss. Maybe it's a tattoo, like mine: *Wingardium Leviosa*, with a swish and a flick. Or maybe it's a mantra, a prayer, a memento of curses past.

Say it, believe it, invoke it, receive it. Ink it into your skin, into your memory. Let it be the light that guides you through the darkness, the light that lifts you up, the light that brings you home.

Bittersweet

The last night I spent in the apartment on Frederick Street, I sat outside by the fire and cried for what felt like an hour, maybe more. It gets dark so early in November, could have been 7 pm, could have been midnight. Could have been another timeline, another dimension altogether.

At some point, I cried so hard that I exploded into laughter. It wasn't subtle at all—it was violent, it was sacred, it was...*surrender*.

For three years, that apartment was home. And while they were only three, a small number, a blip in the cosmos, they completely *transformed* me. They broke me open and exposed the rawest parts of me—the parts that were hiding magic, the parts that were a spell.

Skin after skin after skin I shed, in those three years, within those walls. I'm almost certain that I cried more times in those three than in the previous thirty three combined.

Among the many things I explored in the apartment on Frederick Street, *death* was the most prominent. Not the death of life, necessarily, but the death of things that no longer serve, the death of things that keep us small, the death of that which suffocates the soul.

I learned to let dead things die.

In the wake of that, I learned how to receive.

I had never known, until then, what it meant to receive love and support in healthy ways—from myself, from my people, from the collective. I opened a channel that was clear enough to receive messages from the Universe, and through that channel I created art—the kind of art that finally felt like me, the kind of art that felt like breathing.

I became, in the apartment on Frederick Street, a version of myself that is wholly unashamed. Unapologetic. Unfettered by the burdens of the status quo or the ghosts of my past.

I thought of these ghosts, of the cords I'd cut and the skins I'd shed, as I stared into the barely burning embers of the final backyard fire. And as I wept for the ghosts and the graves and the gossamer scales I'd thrown into the fire on nights antecedent, what I felt most was a flood of **bittersweetness**.

How sweet to know that a heart can heal, how bitter when it breaks. How sweet to know you've grown so much that you've outgrown a thing or two—and still, a tinge of bitter when you turn to say goodbye.

How bitter and how sweet to break so fully open that nothing sinister can survive—to expand beyond the walls of this home into something else entirely.

I swam in that bittersweetness and I felt every drop of it flow through me. What an odd and extraordinary thing it is to swim in the bittersweet, to surrender to the depths of it, to let it fill your lungs.

It washed over me, and I wept. I wept into the fire and I wept to completion—for the many nights I sat in this very same spot, gazing up at the moon, a glass of wine in my hand, a faint whisper of hope within my bones.

Human

You are human, and that's sometimes a hard thing to be. It's hard here, in this human place, and it doesn't always make sense. It can be messy here—chaotic, lackluster, lonely. It can be downright unbearable at times, or at least it feels that way.

But it can be magic, too.

Because here's the thing—you're human, yes. That much is true. But damnit, you're cosmic, too. And it's the cosmic stuff that's going to pull you through, when it's heavy, when it's hard.

When you reach down into the depths of you—past the flesh, past the bone, past the parts of you that will die and return to the earth—there's stardust there.

There is a portal that connects you to the whole of existence, a relic of your time amongst the stars, a reminder that you are not alone in this human place. That you are so much more than this suit of skin, this bag of blood, this walking pile of aches and pains.

You are so much more than a list of to-do's, a number on a scale, a name on a placard, a body on a floating rock in infinite space.

It's like Yoda said: "Luminous beings are we, not this crude matter."

You are of this world just as much as you are of the Universe that surrounds it, and you must never forget your celestial origins. Because when it gets hard here—and it will, in perpetuity—you'll need to reach into that portal, into that cosmic chasm of light and luminance, and hold tightly to the parts of you that this world can never break.

It will try to break you—this human place, where things are hard—and every single time, you will fight to remain whole.

You'll forget sometimes, and that's okay too. You'll hustle to meet deadlines and make dollar signs. You'll question your worth and compare your *everything* to everyone else's. You'll sink into the dark and dreary hole of this human place where magic barely breathes.

You'll say yes to things that suffocate your soul.

When this happens, you'll need to interrupt the pattern. You'll need a metaphorical (perhaps physical) slap to the face. You'll need to do something or go somewhere that snaps you out of it—some place where the lungs of magic expand fully and freely. Some place where celestial whispers can still be heard.

Go to the oceans. Go to the mountains. Go to the quiet

places where the sun paints the sky and human things are sparse, if not unseen—the places where stars shine brighter than anything made by human hands.

Look to the light of the moon. Look to the light within you.

Mine

I went to our coffee shop this morning for the first time since he left.

I've been avoiding it, dreading it, really. Will it hurt? Will I cry? Will they ask me where he is? Where we've been? Am I ready to face it? Am I willing to try?

I'm not sure that I wanted to go, but I know that I needed to, because it's *not* ours, not anymore. I needed to reclaim that space, as I have so many others in the wake of this loss. I needed to know that I could take it back, if I wanted it. If I felt that it were mine.

So much of breaking up is like this: what was ours becomes mine.

What was two becomes one. Things once shared and sacred become solitary, and that's just part of the deal. I don't want to run from these things. I don't want to lose my favorite coffee shop because of him. I don't want to switch gyms. I don't want to stop listening to Radiohead and watching *Rick and Morty*.

I don't want to lose myself. I only want to find myself again.

I want to live my life on my own terms, nothing stolen, nothing lost, because of him.

When people leave, they take so much. What's left when they're gone...well, that's what we have to sort through. Choose what to keep and what to toss, make a pile for each.

It wasn't as heavy as I'd imagined it would be, in that coffee shop that was once ours and is now mine. I cried, as I predicted I would, but in a way that felt a little bit like letting go, a lot like reclamation. I remembered how it felt to sit there across from him the first time we went, the note he passed me, a poem he'd written during our incipient stages of bliss.

I put the coffee shop in the "keep" pile, along with other things I've claimed for myself. I know I'll have to sort through the pile again, face memories and relive moments—but I'll leave that for another day.

Today I'll drink that good good coffee, and celebrate one more thing I didn't let him take from me.

Bleed

What I know about love is that it doesn't have to make you bleed.

It doesn't have to break you, bind you, make you hungry, make you weep.

But sometimes it will.

Sometimes it slices you right open, with it's daggers, with it's deeds. Sometimes you think yourself a victim of love, a hostage, a casualty.

And maybe that isn't love at all. Maybe it looks like love and it talks like love, but it's actually attachment, addiction, or one of their demon cousins.

And maybe you're meant to learn from the bloodshed— to grow in the sticky heartspace of oozing wounds, to stitch them together as you give yourself the love you deserve.

What I know about love is that it's not meant to break you, but sometimes it will try. And even in the face of that, you will remain whole.

Wait

I can't tell you how many times I checked my phone that day.

He was the first guy I'd felt an *ounce* of interest in after the breakup that sent me to the depths of myself. Breaking up is weird; two people merge into one and then break into two again, but there's still remnants. Residuals. Ghost traces of another person embedded in your fibers.

And then, when you're as ready as you'll ever be, you allow yourself to open to another person's energy— but you're not the same you that you were the last time you did this. You've shed skins and cut cords. You've had the chance to choose hope or become jaded, to *address* trauma or *suppress* trauma.

You've got more wrinkles, more scars.

You've traveled through a healing portal, and this version of you only exists because of what you experienced with *another person*. They're not part of your life anymore, but they're still part of *you*. And so you open this new version of you to someone who is also new, and things can be *confusing*.

But I'm getting ahead of myself.

He was the first person who sparked something within me, in the wake of my heartbreak and the healing that followed. When love is lost you feel, for a time, that you might not ever love again. It feels like the truest thing, until it isn't—until someone new enters your atmosphere and reminds you of your infinite capacity to open your heart. That your heart knows how to do this, all on its own.

We were honest about what we were looking for, what we wanted from one another. We agreed not to play games, confirmed that we were on the same page, spoke candidly about our desires. Our conversations were playful and frequent.

Until they weren't.

Until one day—the day I checked my phone too many times—he didn't respond or reach out with his typical frequency. He was silent, on his end of the text dimension.

It didn't matter how many times I checked my phone, the result was the same: nothing. So, naturally, I didn't freak out at all, assumed he was busy, and casually went on with my life.

JUST KIDDING OF COURSE I FREAKED OUT.

Of *course* I wasn't chill. Of course I made up stories in my head. Of course I questioned every single thing right down to the meaning of life itself. Of course I stalked his Instagram for signs of life.

Of course I checked my phone obsessively; what else was I supposed to do?

"You could wait," I said to myself. "You could stay grounded in reality, choose not to spin tales, not to spiral. Don't ruminate. Don't invent worst case scenarios. Just *wait*."

Not a bated breath sort of waiting, but a patient one—a waiting that feels composed and collected. A waiting that looks like business as usual—*life*, uninterrupted.

The kind of waiting that comes from trusting the Universe to provide, in the ways it sees fit, on a timeline of its own. The kind of waiting that teaches us how to flow, how to be present with life, just as it is in this moment. This kind of waiting isn't something we do willingly or very well at all.

Waiting offers an empty space, and in empty spaces there is room for all manner of ghosts and goblins. Empty spaces are vulnerable. Empty spaces are a breeding ground for anxious minds. In the emptiness of waiting, speculation swells. We assume the worst. We assign meaning where meaning is perhaps not necessary.

We create realities that have yet to exist and may never exist at all.

But we don't *have* to fill the empty spaces in this way; it's not the only option. We're capable of navigating these empty spaces without apprehension. We can wait without making assumptions or attaching to outcomes. We can wait and be steady. We can wait and be whole. We can wait for things to unfold without panicking.

We can wait, and through the waiting we can learn about trust, about acceptance.

This is the hardest thing, of course—to wait in this way. To navigate uncertainty without trying to escape it. To exist in the liminal space without a foothold, without armor. Like all things that offer the capacity for growth, waiting is a practice. It's a skill that can be honed, with repetition and consistency. The more we learn to wait, the less resistance we feel towards waiting. Everything gets easier, after awhile.

And so I waited. Hour after hour, without a text, without a word, I waited. I wrote and I sketched and I watched *The Princess Bride*, again. I stayed present with uncertainty. I thought about how it would feel to be the kind of person who didn't rush through liminal spaces. I did my best impression of that kind of person.

I sat in the sticky discomfort without urgency, without angst. It wasn't as stoic as it sounds; it was imperfect and inconsistent, to be sure. I talked my inner cynic into many things and out of many others. I needed constant reminders to wait, but it was waiting, nonetheless.

When the waiting was over, I found parts of myself transmuted. I wasn't the same version of myself that I'd been when the waiting began, because that's what happens when we choose alchemy as a way of existence. After the waiting, because of the waiting, I was a little less controlling, a little more controlled.

There is a part of me that sees the shape of all things—a part of you that does the same—a sliver of the soul that understands the language of the Universe, that is calm enough to hear it when it speaks. That's the part of me that grew, while I waited. That's the part that sets us free.

Listen

I don't always want to listen to the Universe.

I don't want to be told "there's a reason" why my heart had to break again, why things didn't work out the way I'd planned. Sometimes I can do without the platitudes. Sometimes I want to be justified in my angst, left to wallow in the kind of pity that feels entitled. Sometimes I want to stay angry, stay petty, stay halfway hollowed out.

So sometimes, I dismiss the messages, out of petulance, out of contempt.

Sometimes the Universe speaks—in whispers, in signs. And sometimes it screams; sometimes it sends us big, bright, red flags.

And we ignore them. We *resent* them.

Because honestly, *honestly*? It's exhausting.

Lesson after lesson, layer after layer, level after level— the Universe *teaches* and it *takes*. And while we are indeed *here*, doing the work, doing our best to become higher expressions of ourselves by listening, learning, and leveling up, sometimes it just gets old. It's played out. It's redundant.

WE GET IT, okay?

Can we just *live*?

And herein lies the most important lesson of all.

Because the best time to listen to the universe—the times when it really counts, when we need the messages most—is when we're so lost, so weary, so bone tired and nearly broken, that the last thing we want to do is LISTEN TO THE DAMN UNIVERSE.

We want to close ourselves off to the force, and the force pushes back.

It reminds us that yes, there is a purpose to this pain. Yes, you are being tested. Yes, you are being asked to chip away at things that don't support your highest expansion. No, you're not in control. No, your life won't go as planned. And no, *you're not alone.*

The whole of the cosmos, the collective subconscious, the covens past and present have your back. We're all here to reach our hands into the abyss, to grab a hold of you and remind you that you are not alone in this uncertain place.

You are not alone in your grief, in your sorrow, in your rage—in your desire to rebel against the lessons.

We're here to encourage you to *listen*.

Listen. When it's hard, when it's heavy, when you're all but fed up.

Listen. When you're drained, when you're shattered, when you're reaching the end of your rope.

Listen. Even and especially when you don't want to. Because this is when you need it most. This is when you're about to break through.

Ease

The first time I caught my ex-husband cheating was the *hardest* of all the times.

Maybe because it was such a shock—the first inclination that things weren't turning out the way they were "supposed to," that he wasn't the man I thought he was. Or maybe because, as time ticked on, I became desensitized to his antics, and they came to hurt less and less.

Either way, I was *devastated*. Emotionally overwhelmed. Unsure of how to move forward. Frustrated with my inability to just cut the damn cord and call it quits. Going to therapy alone, and together.

Let's just say it was a *rough time* and leave it at that, because this story isn't about him. *My* story isn't about him.

During this difficult time, a colleague reached out, not knowing my situation, and asked how I was doing.

I don't like to answer that question insincerely, so I shared with her that things were hard at the moment—that I was having a tough go at life. To which she responded, "What if it didn't have to be hard? What if it could be *easy*?"

This bitch!

She had no idea what I was going through, no concept of the depths of my pain, and she was suggesting it should be...easy? I was *enraged*.

I felt entitled to my pain, valid in my experience, and righteous in my anger. What I was going through was hard—that much was universally understood.

Who was *she* to tell me it could be *easy*?

In the five years since that exchange, my life has changed so much that I don't recognize the version of myself who took offense to her suggestion. I got divorced, eventually. Later, I met someone new, loved him more completely than I've ever loved another, and broke into pieces when he left me two years later.

And then, of course, I came back together more whole, more supple—and I've been rising from the ashes ever since, finding magic in the shadows once again.

In these five years since, I overcame the kind of fears that kept me small: the fear of sharing my art with the world, the even greater fear of publicly identifying as a witch, and so many others in the same vein. I reclaimed the worthiness and power that was always mine and never up for debate.

I finally stopped straightening my hair and came to an agreement with my curls.

I learned to ask for help without shame, embraced my salty disposition without apology, shed so many skins, and watched my baby become a teenager.

But most of all, I learned about *ease*.

I learned that even when there is chaos, even when there is struggle, even when your heart hurts and your bones ache, *you can feel ease*.

I learned that even in the depths of despair, you can find magic.

I learned how to laugh at Cosmic Jokes.

I learned that the Universe is Trolling me—that in order to accept my blessings and my deepest levels of expansion, I needed to also accept that I was being pranked, that we're all being pranked.

And I learned that those *pranks* were actually *gifts*. This is how we are nourished, time and time again.

I think back on that conversation years ago and realize that I had misunderstood the concept of ease, at least in this context. I'd presumed that choosing ease meant invalidating my pain, condoning the behavior of the one who'd hurt me.

I thought "ease" was akin to being flippant and naive— that it was something reserved for flaky folks who didn't live on planet Earth, like the rest of us.

I didn't understand that ease was actually just *trust*.

Everything in life is ephemeral.

Life is fleeting. Sometimes it hurts. Sometimes it makes no sense. And then sometimes, everything clicks and it's just...*magic*.

Trust is knowing you can have that magic feeling within you any time you choose, even and especially when the walls around you are crumbling.

Trust is knowing the Universe will nourish you, if you let it do so in its own way.

Trust is loosening your grip, and do you know what happens when you loosen your grip?

You experience *ease*. You breathe, for what feels like the first time.

You realize that nothing is as serious as we think it is, and that while our pain is valid, and while life is sometimes hard and heavy, we *can* let go, just a little bit at a time.

We can exhale. We can laugh. We can drop our collective shoulders, unclench our universal jaw. We can lay down our swords. We can take action without trying to *control outcomes*. We can have hope without also having expectations.

We can trust ourselves to experience ease.

Whatever

I've done a lot of things I never thought I would do.

Things don't always turn out the way you imagine, your priorities shift, your lens of the world is altered, your ideas of what is possible are constantly being challenged.

If you'd have asked me five years ago about the trajectory of my professional life, I would have told you I'd be writing books, but they wouldn't have been the books I went on to write. I certainly wouldn't have predicted I'd be reading Tarot for people across the globe.

If you'd have asked me on this day last year, if I'd be spending my Saturday night alone, crying into a glass of wine while suffering through the second season of *Twin Peaks* that we never finished together, I would have probably laughed in your face.

But here I sit, in a bed that is now mine and no longer ours, watching Agent Cooper play a deadly game of chess, living the life that no one planned.

We think we know what's coming, or who we're going to be. We're foolish enough to believe we can plan ahead and the Universe will abide. We're wrong a lot of the time, probably more than we're right.

I've lived so many lives within this lifetime, been a chameleon, a shapeshifter, worn multiple hats, found myself in situations I swore I'd never be in, enjoying things I used to hate, rejecting things I used to swear by.

So now, instead of saying "never" I say "whatever, forever." Anything can happen. Everything can change. All of it is temporary, anyway. Shed one skin, slither into another. Over and over again, because the snake eats it's own tail, every single time.

A circle has no beginning and no end.

Who are we to fight this?

Who are we to arrange the pieces of a puzzle that has no edges, to play a game that has no rules? Who are we to be so rigid in a world where everything is malleable, where uncertainty is the only thing that's guaranteed?

Pause

Being an adult isn't what any of us thought it would be.

Growing up watching *Three's Company* reruns, and later, *Seinfeld* and *Friends*, my expectations of adulthood were a lot more exciting, a lot less mundane.

Yet here we are, doing adult things with adult problems, paying adult bills, checking off adult boxes. The truth is, being an adult can be cumbersome. It can wear on you, tear on you, take the breath right out of you.

Maybe you're *tired*. Maybe your feet hurt and your bones ache and your eyes aren't as sharp as they used to be. Maybe you find yourself grunting and groaning every time you get up.

Maybe you question whether or not you've lived the life you planned to live. Maybe you look back and wonder where the time went, how it all got swallowed up. How you got to be so grown.

Maybe it feels like life is just *one thing after the other*, an endless to-do list of nothing and everything, all at once. Maybe it feels like you can never pause and catch your breath, and it's when you feel this that way that pausing is the most important thing.

Pause. Reflect. Take a break from the hustle to see just how far you've come, how much you've reaped because of what you sowed. Your blessings will never feel like enough if you don't pause to call them in. Your load will always feel too heavy if you never set it down.

This is a time for checking your compass. For correcting your course and adjusting your third eye. This is a time to *celebrate*, even if it feels premature, especially if it feels undeserved. Lay an offering at the foot of your labor.

Honor the parts of you that you've shed, the parts of you that you've *shared*, the parts of you that you've *nurtured* into their fullness.

Dissect the parts of you that refuse to pause; ask your soul what it needs to thrive within it's grown up body. Question your commitment to the hustle. Unmap yourself from capitalism. Detach from the grind.

Because the truth is, being an adult doesn't have to be a grind. The hustle is not required. These are manufactured half-truths, designed to keep the cogs in the wheel, our dreams always slightly out of reach. The *overculture* profits from convincing us that we aren't working hard enough, and we've got to hustle harder.

The overculture doesn't want us to pause, because if we do, we'll discover how much we've *already* done, how far we've *actually* come. We'll shift our focus away from our losses onto our wins. We'll recognize that our capacity for abundance far outweighs the mindset of scarcity we've been conditioned to uphold.

And so, despite our cultural proclivity towards upward mobility at all costs, you've got to give yourself permission to pause. Give thanks for the way you've tended the earth, for the sweat you've poured into the soil, for the tears you've shed in the process of your own personal alchemy.

This is the way you will keep going, the sustenance that will foster your journey and keep you moving in the direction of your highest good.

Resist

I will do *anything* to avoid writing.

In truth, the only thing at which I'm more skilled than writing is *not writing*—hiding from writing, running from writing, going to great lengths to get out of writing.

Laundry, dishes, plant care, and closet organization never seem more appealing than when a writing deadline looms.

Suddenly, I have to floss.

I just remembered, I need to color code my bookshelf. And most importantly, I need to stare at Instagram for hours. This step cannot be skipped.

But damnit I can only avoid it for so long. Writing is what I was put on this earth to do—it's woven into the very fabric of my being. It's cellular, it's in my marrow. Nothing feels as good as my fingers across a keyboard. Nothing feels as right.

And so, when I finally sit down to do it, I'm uncomfortable at first. I resist. I fight. Until it consumes me, engulfs me, ensorcels me—*and I am home.*

It's like that sometimes, with the things that bring me home. Every time I get on my mat and stretch, I think, "Damn, I need to do this more." Every hike, every sunset, every camping trip I wonder, "How has it been so long since the last time I came to worship at the feet of the Great Mother?"

These are the things that bring me home to myself, and so of course, I resist them. Anything that is in pursuit of my magic will be accompanied by resistance, because that's just part of the deal—the more I gravitate towards my higher self, the more resistance tries to hold me back.

I'm a celestial being, having a human experience, as are you. This truth about our existence is undoubtedly remarkable, yet equally problematic. The celestial part of you perpetually seeks expansion, but the human part of you often gets in the way—with excuses, with obligations, with to-do lists, with fear.

It's a tug of war between what's cosmic and what's conditioned, between the magic and the mundane. If you want to feel absolutely alive—to be at home within your body, your soul, down to the stardust in your bones—your cosmic nature has to win this fight, again and again.

We are born with so much primal magic in our hearts,

and as we grow older, crushed beneath the sheer gravity of adulthood, we *forget*. The calling of our soul, once raw and raucous, fades into a whisper.

Resistance creeps in and keeps us from answering that call. It brings with it doubt and depletion—it comes in the forms of imposter syndrome, cynicism, and procrastination. It's armed with endless distractions, a myriad reasons to stay in the grind, in the *Matrix*.

Resistance is strong, but the magic within you is stronger.

Your task is to nurture that magic: water it, tend to its earth, give it everything it needs to transmute light energy into chemical energy into the alchemy of your celestial soul. Feed your cosmic tendencies. Arm yourself with spells. When resistance comes—because it always does—you'll be ready.

You'll be poised for the fight.

Traffic

Los Angeles traffic is a special kind of hell.

If you'd like to travel 2 miles across town during rush hour, I sure hope you've allotted 90 minutes to do so. I sure hope you've got provisions and the kind of music that was made for driving.

And if you need to take the 405, for anything, anywhere, any time—you have my condolences.

We know this, and we choose it. Because in choosing Los Angeles, we're choosing other things, too. I was born and raised in the City of Angels, and while I don't plan on dying here, I'm choosing it now—for the weather, the art, the culture, the food, the mountains, the beaches, and of course, the sunsets.

Especially the Autumn sunsets, when the clouds are thick and the sun makes a canvas of the sky. Especially at the beach, when that canvas is unobstructed by human things like buildings and billboards and cars, cars, cars. Especially without the honking. The incessant honking.

It was a Wednesday in November, driving home in heavy traffic, bombarded by the sound of honking horns, when I decided I needed to make more time for sunsets. Specifically, more time for sunsets at the beach.

Because despite the chaos all around me, the sky was at peace.

Red and gold and stretched infinitely into the cosmos, the sky was a message. The sky was a spell. It crept into my bones and loosened all the tight things within me, melting me into the driver's seat of my jeep, bringing me back to my cosmic roots.

And as I breathed it in—the magic of our Great Mother, the serenity that only nature can bring—I couldn't help but wish I was consuming it without the clutter. Without the rage of nearby motorists, the tangle of power wires that swept across the sky. I wished I was sitting on the beach, wrapped in a blanket, my bare feet against the cold November sand.

I wanted this sunset in its fullness, to watch our planet's star dip beneath the Pacific, a symphony of waves, a bastion of salt.

I wanted more sunsets and less traffic. Period.

The next morning, as I read the Tarot and wrote in my journal, I made a list of promises to myself, promises I intend to keep. One such promise was to watch the sunset from the beach at least once every lunar cycle, preferably when the moon is full and the tides are at their lowest.

I know that traffic—which is to say, adulthood—is inevitable. I know my to-do lists aren't getting any shorter. I know my books won't write themselves, my bills won't pay themselves, my load will only lighten if I do the heavy lifting.

I'm realistic. I know that much as I yearn to live under a canopy of stars, in some faraway place where things are yet unspoiled, I'm not there yet. I'm here, in this city, in this traffic, in this life that is sometimes a bustle, a hustle, a calendar of chores.

But I also know those things can wait.

The tedium of life abides, but each sunset is ephemeral—this is transient magic, the kind we have to capture before it's gone forever. If I want it, I know where to find it. If I want it, I have to go and get it. I've got to tinker with time, find pockets where sunsets and sunrises and star gazing can be penciled in, here and there, as needed, as the schedule allows.

That's a promise I can make. That's a promise I can keep.

Manifest

I want to wake up early.

And because I want to wake up early, I *say* I want to wake up early. I say it to myself, to my son, to the Universe, to my journal. I say I want to rise before the sun, to drink my coffee in silence, in stillness. I say I want to consult my Tarot cards and whisper spells into the cosmos, before the calm turns to bustle, before the day grows full and frantic.

I say this, because I *really* do want this. I am most alive in those early morning hours. It is and always has been when I'm most creative—when my magic is at its most tangible.

The kind of magic I'm seeking only exists in the hours that bookend the dawn. There's a part of me that doesn't breathe except within this frame of time—the part that has the answers to all my own questions, the part that isn't frayed at the edges, the part that doesn't rush.

I want to be still with her, that part of me. To have coffee with her, to sit on the balcony with her and listen to the birds with her. I want to access her as often as she'll allow. I want that so damn badly, but I don't always act like it.

Sometimes I act in ways that take me further away from her. Sometimes I act in direct opposition of what I say I want to manifest.

Some nights, instead of lights out at 9 or 9:30 or even 10—bedtime hours that would allow me to rise restfully with the sun—I lie awake staring at my phone, or I pull out my laptop because I forgot to do something seemingly urgent.

It's true that sometimes what keeps me awake is something that matters, something with the capacity for expansion—a creative flow that I dare not interrupt, a book that has captured my breath within its pages. But most often, even those things can wait.

And so, when I wake to the sounds of rush hour traffic outside my window, I am often disappointed, but never surprised. I can't possibly expect to manifest the things I want if my actions and intentions are at odds.

Manifestation, after all, is simply an intersection.

It's the place where action and intention meet to discuss terms. It's the overlap of what we want, and what we're willing to do to get it. It's the secret wishes of our hearts, set into motion with our hands, carried out in the fullness of time because we gave them what they needed in order to thrive.

Without intention—which is to say, our dreams, our hopes, our desires—we'd be *lost*. Without purpose. Without longing. Without clarity. Without cause.

But without action, these hopes and desires will remain as such. They will not be transmuted from dreams to reality, and they will gnaw at you until you either *suppress* them or *support* them.

The Universe answers to those who show up to collaborate. It favors action. It supports the dreamers who are also *doers*.

But, when we fail to cooperate, when we misalign our actions and intentions, when we do the exact opposite of what our wishes require—it doesn't turn its back. Instead, it continues to give us opportunities to realign. It sends messages, in bottles, on rolled up parchment, with ravens, with owls.

It whispers until it wails. It does not appreciate being ignored.

It *wants* to give you the magic you're seeking. It yearns to help you achieve your dreams. It only asks that you act in accordance with the wishes you've made—that you show up and do some of the heavy lifting, too.

At the very least, it asks that you refrain, as often as you can, from sending mixed messages—from saying one thing, and doing another.

If you want it, say you want it, act like you want it, believe that you'll get it, and the Universe will oblige.

Start

If you want to get somewhere—anywhere—you really just need to *start*. You only need to do one thing, and the thing after that, subsequently. Then, simply keep doing that, over and over.

You don't need to do *all* the things at once, or ever, actually. You don't even need to do all the things "perfectly" either. You don't need to worry about the end result, or stress over possible outcomes of which you have no control.

Just start with one step. And the next step. And the step after that. Each step helps you build momentum, and I'm not sure there's anything more powerful than momentum when it comes to the process of creating or achieving or doing anything at all.

Starting is the key to everything.

But when it's time to begin, we often *don't*.

We find ourselves completely overwhelmed by where

to start, how to start, and all of the myriad things that could possibly go wrong once we do. We stare at blank pages, consumed by imposter syndrome. We stand in front of fresh canvases, burdened by doubts. We sit at cluttered desks and work benches, inundated with options, overcome with dread.

We will think of every excuse not to start.

We'll deliberately become distracted by other things—things that perhaps (and most likely) require less startup energy. We'll have 22 browser tabs open instead of just the one. We'll watch 11 episodes of a show we've already seen.

Starting is hard.

In fact, it's the hardest.

It takes more effort to start than it does to continue. Hell, the only thing that compares to starting is *finishing*, but we'll leave that for another day.

Today, we'll focus on the threshold, **as if it's the only thing that exists**. All you need to do is step through it, onto the other side, into the realm of action, and let momentum take your hand.

Starting is a potion. Starting is a portal. Starting will set you on a path, any path, which is better than standing around agonizing over which direction to go and what will happen when you get there (what will happen if you don't?).

Because when you start, when you drink the potion

and step through the portal, you'll find it easier to continue. Resistance will fade into the background. The worried parts of you will wither. The doubts will dissolve. The path will appear.

Start now. Start again. Start slowly or quickly, with a bang or with a whisper. *Just start.*

That's the first thing, for now.

Finish

I'm currently the author of three unfinished books—
four, if you count this one. Five if you count the one
I've been writing in my head.

I can't tell you how many times I've uttered the words,
"Why am I like this," to myself, to my Tarot cards, to
the void—but this is what I do. I start and I start and
I start...and I struggle to *finish*.

Maybe it's because I get excited, and I start too many
things at once. They fragment me, my many projects,
my myriad paths. It's true that doing multiple things
at once can be a distraction, dividing your attention
and delaying the process of completion. Multitasking
doesn't really live up to its name—instead, it causes
most tasks to be left *incomplete*.

But maybe, just maybe, finishing is actually terrifying.

Maybe struggling to finish is a form of perfectionism.
Of resistance. Of hiding. Maybe avoiding the finish is
a way to protect myself. Maybe finishing makes me

vulnerable. Maybe finishing means I will stand naked in the light, for all the world to see.

And maybe, if I don't finish, I'll never have to let myself be seen. If my words never etch themselves onto paper, if you never hold that paper in your hands, I'll be safe. No can touch me here in the shelter of my art studio, behind the shield of my laptop.

There are so many reasons we fail to finish, some of them valid, others not so much.

Sometimes *instead* of finishing, it's better to walk away—but this message isn't about those times. **This message is about those things that dreams are made of**. The things you *want* to finish. The things you *need* to finish. The things your soul begs you to bring to fruition, to completion. The things that feel like *breathing*.

There are so many reasons not to finish those things, too.

These reasons are less valid, and more sinister.

They come to you in whispers—not from the cosmos, but from decrepit places, deceptive places. These reasons are born of the shadows, and they are harbingers of doom. They will, if given the opportunity, obstruct your process and impede your growth.

They will go to great lengths to keep you small, because this is how they survive.

And you've got to fight them—these little demons,

these creatures of the dark. You've got to send them back to the shadows from whence they came. Bind them. Block them. Cast a spell to hold their tongues.

Because in order to walk the path of your heart, you need to finish. In order to do the alchemy of your soul, you need to finish. In order to share your gifts with the collective, to make an offering to the cosmos, to send your deepest exhale into the void, you need to finish.

It will never be perfect, because nothing ever is.

It might be chipped and cracked and frayed at the edges—but as long as it's complete, it has the potential to satisfy your soul.

Portals

Most things aren't perfect, and I don't want them to be.

I'm here for the messy, the mangled, the misshaped and the mashed up. I'm not interested in straight lines and polished silver.

But there are a handful of things in this world that are close to perfect—there are portals to bliss, in the everyday, in the seemingly mundane.

A morning cup of coffee is one of those portals, for me. Before the sun heats the concrete of this corpulent metropolis, before the day has its way with me, this potent elixir brings me moments of peace within myself, heats up the magic in my bones.

There are other portals, too—in rainbows that splash apartment walls, in songs that play like incantations. There are things that may seem commonplace, but that doesn't make them any less miraculous.

I hope you seek these portals. I hope you see them, too, when they're seeking you. I hope you find them. I hope you enter, as a ritual, as a rite.

Bottle

The thing about writing is that I don't do it because I want to.

I mean, I *do* want to, don't get me wrong. The entire process of writing feels like home to me. I like the way it feels to scratch a pen to paper, just as much as I like punching the sticky keys of my vintage Smith Corona. I've often been accused of being a "loud typist," even on the smooth keyboard of a modern laptop, but that's just what happens when I get excited. I type aggressively. I type with abandon.

I *love* writing, but that's not why I do it. I write because I *have* to.

For me, writing feels like breathing. Sometimes the breath is shallow and terse, but other times my lungs expand and contract with the stroke of the keyboard.

I've *always* known I needed to write. It has called to me, from the depths of my soul, since I was very young. The times when I didn't answer that call—because I was distracted, disjointed, disobedient—these were the times I felt least like myself.

Writing—or any kind of creative self expression—is like putting a message in a bottle, throwing it out into the atmosphere, and hoping someone feels something when they find it, *if* they find it.

Except, the message is your *whole entire soul*.

This is what it's like to create—to do anything at all that exposes you, anything that allows you to be seen. It's terrifying and vulnerable and you do it anyway, because you *must*. Because not doing it is worse. Because if you don't do it, you won't be yourself.

Because if you don't do it, you won't be able to *stand* yourself.

Because it screams at you from within. It thrashes. It claws. It needs to come out.

Of course, it won't always be easy to release the thing that claws from within—to do the thing that makes you feel most like yourself. Sometimes you'll have to bleed for it. Sometimes you'll have to get dirty, get sweaty, stretch yourself to the very edges of your own existence.

Whatever it takes to get that message out of your body and into its bottle, is what you've got to do. Even when it hurts to do it, even when it's scary, even if it seems like no one cares at all and none of it matters and what's the damn point—you have to do it. You just *have* to.

It's not called the Soul's Purpose for nothing.

We worry so much about what might happen if we write our messy little spells on scraps of paper, and stuff those paper scraps into washed out pickle jars, the labels carefully removed, the lids tightly fastened.

We worry that no one will find the jars, the bottles, the spells we've cast out into the void. That no one will read the messages. That if they *do* find the bottles and they do read the messages, they'll toss them or trash them or judge them or worse yet, pretend like they never read them at all.

So even through the thrashing and the clawing and the clanging and the banging, we find reasons to keep the magic to ourselves—hidden away in secret places that no one else can see.

What we *really* should be worrying about is what will happen if we don't let the magic out—what will happen if we allow ourselves to be clawed at from the inside until we sleep eternally, until we cross the veil.

And so I write—not because I want to, even though I want to. I write because refusing to write is like refusing to breathe. Because the fear of keeping my magic locked away is worse than the fear of what will happen if I unleash it.

Because there are so many bottles to fill, so why not be someone who fills them?

Curls

I know that I haven't straightened my hair in six months because I know it's been six months since he left. There's no direct correlation between the two, except that they coincidentally coincided.

Or maybe it wasn't a coincidence at all, seeing as how both of these things have led me back home to myself. Maybe I lost myself in him. Maybe this is part of my healing process—the reclamation of myself in whatever shape it takes.

For now, let's just talk about the curls.

My entire life, I lamented my curls. I fought with my curls. I apologized for my curls. I straightened my curls.

I can still conjure a vision of seventh grade me, kneeling on the bathroom floor, a sheet over the toilet seat, using a *laundry iron* to straighten my waist length hair.

I was desperate for straight hair.

Hair straightening irons didn't become a household item until much later, but when they did, I had those, too. I've bought every product, tried every method, and even did a chemical treatment to eradicate the curls that gave me so much trouble.

I *hated* my curls. I thought they were ugly—I thought they made *me* ugly.

But now, six months into reviving them, I am at peace with them, at home with them. Don't get me wrong, some days I *still* hate them—anyone with curls can tell you they do whatever the hell they damn please on any given day. But I don't lament them anymore. I don't try to erase them. And I certainly don't apologize for them.

There are so many things I don't apologize for anymore—so many parts of me I've shed that weren't ever mine to begin with. So many things I've reclaimed through the process of shedding. So many burdens I've set down, only after realizing they were never mine to carry. Because we're carrying so much, aren't we? So much that isn't ours?

No matter how many of these things I shed, I continue to find more. I've been doing the work—the healing, the learning, the unlearning—for so many years. Yet still, so much remains.

So many layers to unravel, unpack, unburden.

Narratives, roles, attachments, convictions. Some

of them I choose to shed, others are taken from me without my consent. None of them were mine. None of them were home.

One by one, the Universe clears the path. One by one, the way home becomes less cluttered. One by one, the things that don't belong to us are crushed, like horcruxes beneath the Sword of Griffyndor—but only if we wield that sword, only if we're brave enough to let them go.

It will be uncomfortable, of that much you can be sure.

It'll be work, hard work, like bringing dead curls back to life or letting other dead things die. You'll have to look at everything you're holding and ask if it's really yours—examine your entire concept of reality to see if it needs to be disrupted, dismantled, reframed.

And just when you think you've figured it out, you'll find one more thing to shed, one more layer to peel back.

This is the way home.

Keep going.

Panic

If you know anything about houseplants, then you know the Fiddleleaf Fig is *kind of an asshol*e.

In the wild, *Ficus Lyrata* absolutely *thrives*. Indigenous to West Africa, it grows to enormous proportions in dense rainforests, with no help from humans, thank you very much.

Once domesticated, however, it's finicky as hell.

Too much sun.

Not enough sun.

Too wet.

Too dry.

Mist for humidity.

Avoid cold drafts.

Turn often for chlorophyll balance.

Give it fertilizer but not too much.

Don't let the leaves burn.

Don't let the leaves burn.

Don't let the leaves burn.

You can give a Fiddleleaf Fig the life you *think* it needs and wants, and it may still refuse to cooperate.

My Fiddleleaf Fig has been with me through two long term relationships, two separate homes, and a multitude of struggles. And in that time, Elvira—because that's her name—has had every malady imaginable.

First, because I didn't yet know she needed to rotate, all of the leaves on one side of her trunk fell off. Then, she got spider mites. And then she got them again. Leaves fell and I didn't know. Leaves yellowed and I didn't know why. Leaves turned crispy and I didn't know why, and so on and so forth until forever.

But still, she *survives*, and in doing so, she has taught me a great deal about patience and composure.

Now, when one of her leaves inevitably falls off, I **don't panic**. Instead, I triage the situation. What could have possibly caused this? I go down the list, ruling out some culprits, considering others. And then, with as much calm and curiosity as I can muster, I develop a plan of action.

And because I refuse to panic, I'm able to move forward with clarity and trust. No matter what happens, no matter how this plays out, I know I did the best I could to address the situation because I chose to be *centered* rather than *frazzled*.

Maybe you're on the verge of panic, as so many of us often are.

Maybe you're struggling, or *have* struggled, or *will* struggle as time fulfills its promise. Maybe you've been hit suddenly, hit hard, hit right in the gut. Maybe something unexpected, something unsettling, is fraying your nerves. Maybe you feel shaken, afraid, uncertain.

And maybe, just maybe, you don't have to panic.

Because if you choose *not* to panic, you're choosing to be present—to address your worries with a level head and an open heart. You give your intuition room to breathe. When you panic, you lose your ground. You become untethered. You manifest all manner of possible disastrous outcomes. You step out into the wild without a compass, without a map.

Don't panic.

If you discover a fallen leaf or a bed of bone-dry soil, don't panic. If things get messy and the plan unravels, don't panic. Come back to your body, to your breath. Ask yourself what can be done—devise a plan, be intentional, take action.

When you choose composure over chaos, you send a message to the Universe that says, "I've got this." You throw a vibe out into the cosmos that says, "I'm capable." You accept the challenge. You steady your hands. You sheath your sword and pack your provisions. You ready yourself for what's to come. You trust that you can handle it.

And if it feels impossible to trust, because I know that it will, remember this:

You've been through bad shit and sad shit and scary shit, too. You've climbed mountains that seemed insurmountable, worked through shadows that felt infinite in their darkness, and held the shattered pieces of your heart in your bare, shaking hands.

And *every single time*, you've come through—even when you thought you wouldn't survive, you clawed your way out of each and every abyss. You've risen from the ashes of every fire.

There's no need to panic. There is only your inhale, your exhale, the heart that beats, beats, beats within you. Plant your feet firmly on the ground, realign your third eye, and move forward in the direction of your blessings.

Vanilla

There's always some kind of standard I'm not living up to—a box I'm not checking off, a norm I'm (inadvertently) rebelling against, a construct I'm disrupting. Society expects a woman to be one thing and I am something else completely.

Too loud. Too independent. Too everything and not enough of everything else.

A past version of myself was uncomfortable with this. She questioned her worth because of it. She persistently tried to conform to the standard. She persistently failed. But the version of me that is writing this, the version of me that is whole, the one who's finally at home in her skin, she's okay with it. I'm okay with it.

More than okay with it, really—I'm into it. I am *alive* because of it. Awake. Fully engaged in my *own* life, on my *own* terms.

I'm a muscular woman. An "aggressive" woman. A single mom who doesn't "dress like a mom," whatever the hell that means. I'm a *spiritual* advisor with a *salty* soul and *foul* mouth. I have a lot of opinions and a lot of tattoos.

I am untamed.

Here, in this home that is my body, my heart, my wild, untamed soul, things are mostly unconventional. Here, there are dichotomies and contradictions. There are rules that don't get followed—rules that are decidedly arbitrary, created and upheld by some equally arbitrary authority.

Here there are many flavors. There's vanilla, sure, but there's rocky road, too.

And because I acknowledge this variety of flavors—because I know will never check off all the boxes or fit into their beige and boring expectations of what it means to be a woman identifying person in today's world—I choose, instead, to go my own damn way.

I choose to reject the ceaseless pressure to conform. I choose to write my own stories, in spite of the narratives the Patriarchy has offered. I choose to hold my own standards, and make my own rules.

And I choose to sometimes **break** my rules, when they need to be broken. To revise and amend my rules, as my consciousness expands and my values evolve.

I am completely disinterested in the overculture.*

The overculture lacks appeal.

The overculture is vanilla, at best.

But this life I chose—that I'm choosing—isn't about going against the grain, at least not on purpose. I am not *intentionally* disrupting the status quo. I am simply existing on my own terms against a "grain" that is narrow, limiting, and quite frankly, uninteresting.

Human beings are not one dimensional; we contain multitudes. We are not robots. We are not clones. We are the cosmos, incarnate.

Our life—*this* life—it's not an audition. It doesn't come with a script. Life pushes outward in all directions. It doesn't follow the linear path we've been presented.

Despite this, the overculture maintains the falsehood of some universally agreed upon script that we're all meant to follow. And at some point, because you're fed up, because you're awakening, you become too aware of the script, and you start to go off book.

You wake up and see how sleepy the "standard" truly is—you know you can never be that sleepy again. You're too alive now, in your facets, in your flavors.

You get so far away from the standard that the pressure to conform to it no longer exists. It loses its allure. You connect so deeply to the true aspects of your being—the stuff that's in your marrow, in your guts, in your cosmic DNA—that the standard begins to feel...*substandard.*

It's a lie. You know it's a lie. You witness this deception, and you *recoil* from it. Untether yourself from it. Return to the halcyon home in your heart, where these lies have no power, where these lies cannot breathe.

The lies are absurd to you now. The lies have no luster. The lies say you've got to be *vanilla* if you want to walk this earth with your head up and your heart full—but you know damn well you've got other flavors in your bones.

Overculture: The dominant culture in a society, whose traditions and customs are those normally followed in public, as opposed to a subculture.

Taxes

I don't really know what I'm doing—in business, in motherhood, as a cosmic being navigating this human place we call home. I'm doing my best, that much I know, but I'm not really sure about anything else.

In searching my memory, I cannot recall a single moment in the past 37 years when I didn't feel like I was completely *winging it*.

I've been a single parent since my early 20s, thrust into unplanned parenthood, trying to inflict as little damage as possible to my ancestral line.

Every business decision I've ever made has been done with my *gut*, without extensive planning or any kind of safety net. I don't have a lawyer and I'm pretty sure my accountant secretly hates me for the state of my books.

I've been married *twice*. Divorced *twice*. Left broken hearted more times than I care to recall.

I'm still trying to figure out things like taxes, health insurance, and what that flashing red light on my dashboard means. I can't seem to get air in the left rear tire of my Jeep. I constantly confuse arteries with veins, I have no idea what the pancreas does, and I don't floss nearly as often as I tell my dentist I do.

I've been absolutely overwhelmed with financial, parental, and professional responsibilities. I've had moments when I realized, "OH SHIT, THIS IS ALL ON ME," and marveled at the fact that anyone would let me be in charge of *anything*, when I still don't feel like an actual "grown up."

And despite all of this, I feel as though I'm *exactly* where I'm meant to be—doing my soul's work, walking my sacred path, taking it day by day, sunrise to sunset.

One night, after a particularly challenging day, I confided this in my teenager. I told him, because I always try to tell him the truest things, that I was just *making it up* as I went along. I told him that grown ups don't always know what the hell we're doing—that we make mistakes. We hurt. We heal. We hurt some more. We don't have all the answers, or really many answers at all.

But we can't completely fall apart, even if falling apart seems like the only option, because we're expected to "have it all together." Because **no one is coming to save us.**

"Yeah, that makes sense," he said. He understood. He's sage and sentient in the way that only children can be.

There's this lie we've been told, this lie we've all chosen to believe: that everyone else has it figured out—everyone but us. Kids don't believe this lie, at least not yet.

But we, the grown and wise and mighty, we spend so much time thinking we're the *only* ones whose lives are a total mess. We're the only ones with a sink full of dishes and a stack of unpaid parking tickets. We're the only ones who have to push trash and random objects off the passenger seat so that someone can sit in our car. We're the only ones who kill houseplants. We're the only ones still dealing with acne in our 30s.

We're the only ones who can't seem to get it right.

We waste so much energy on comparison, on shame, on pretending we know what we're doing just so we can seem more adult.

None of us know what we're doing.

We're all just out here, stumbling around in the dark, doing what we feel is maybe our best on any given day. We're all just a little bit confused—as parents. As humans. As healers. As seekers. Most of life is making it up along the way.

There's no singular way to travel through life. There's no framework. We try and *fail* just as much as we try and *succeed*. We fall down. We get back up. We try a different route. We check our compass and course correct. Over and over in the infinite loop of time.

No one has this figured out, even the ones who seem

like they do. Most of our lives are in various states of disarray; most of us are still growing up, growing out of things, growing into ourselves, over and over.

If we can accept that—if we can admit that we're a mess and you're a mess and I'm a mess, too—maybe we'll feel a little less alone, and a little more at *home*. Maybe it'll take the pressure off, and we can all be a mess, together.

Sunset

You had to really want to be there. You had to be seeking something. You had to be willing to receive it, when it came, in whatever shape it came in.

It was cold, to be sure. Cold for California, cold for anywhere. My bare feet were almost numb against the wet November sand. The wind whipped viciously through my hair, piercing my skin, burning through the drums of my ears. There is no mercy on this beach, but there is magic in droves.

The shore wasn't thronged the way it is in Summer.

The ocean carries secrets in these colder months, but not a lot of people know this. And so we were but a handful, a smattering of souls willing to brave the chill, in search of something, in search of anything. I know each of them felt what I felt, in their own unique way, according to their personal pain, their particular wishes.

We were all there to feel it—the way the earth beneath

you settles when the sun creates a still life of cotton candy clouds, the way every cell within you moves in sync with the waves, crashing gently. The tide is low as the day lays itself quietly to rest.

It's only in these moments that everything is still enough, serene enough, to hear those celestial whispers—that our hearts open their chambers and our blood runs clear, that we feel the magic in our marrow, that the Universe speaks and we actually, actually, actually listen.

I listened.

Tonight, it told me that he's starting to feel like a stranger. And that was the truest thing.

Wish

11:33 pm, a Saturday night in December.

I'm sitting on the floor in my art studio, doing inventory, tagging and folding t-shirts that I designed, preparing to launch a new line of screen printed goods the following day.

I say this is my art studio, because it's *supposed* to be my art studio—but there's no room to make art because every surface is covered with merchandise. The merchandise *is* the art, of course, but you get it.

Harry Potter and The Goblet Fire plays in the background, a glass of Seven Moons Red is always within reach. I'm not wearing any pants, and I've just realized I probably won't get to bed for another few hours.

I can't stop smiling.

I wished for this.

This little business of mine that I built from scratch,

the art that I'm making, the goods that I'm slangin'—this Saturday night on the floor in my underwear, it's everything I wished for.

I'm careful not to complain about the labor. I'm conscious of the way my hands approach the work, the way my heart feels at peace here, in this dream that I manifested.

I'm careful, as well, to acknowledge that while some things in my life are kind of a mess, they aren't the only things worthy of my attention. My blessings deserve my attention, too.

I am not the kind of witch who dishes out "love and light," and as such, I won't patronize you with platitudes about the bright side. I find a great deal of value in salt and shadows; I believe we all must endure the dark night of the soul if we are to come into our fullness.

But I also believe that when we snub our blessings, the Universe takes note.

When we focus only—or at least primarily—on the *messes* in our lives, what use have we for the *miracles*? For the magic? If you don't believe in your ability to manifest blessings, in your worthiness to receive them, will you even recognize them when they arrive?

I wished for this art studio full of garments and packaging supplies. I wished for the kind of life where I could create things that set my soul on fire. I wished for the courage to call myself a writer, the audacity to invoke the Muse.

So many of the things I wished for are mine now. So many things are good and pure and true. Not all of life is a dumpster fire. Not everything is trash.

Remember when you wished for the things you have now?

Soundtrack

For the first time in a long time, I woke up and didn't feel like listening to sad songs.

Music is one of the first things I consume each day, along with coffee. It's part of every morning ritual—a record, a playlist, something to set or match the mood. The last several months my musical choices have reflected my healing process—avoidant at first, due to shock, then angry for awhile, and after the anger, a stretch of sadness.

I longed for the anger when it was gone. It was easier to feel the sharpness of the dagger. My anger protected me. My anger gave me shelter and shield. My anger made me feel alive during a time when I was sure I was dying.

The sadness *enveloped* me.

My playlists for October, November, and December were decidedly melancholy—their melodies wistful, their lyrics an infinite loop of sorrow. I needed this sadness, of course; it's all part of the process. I needed the avoidance and the anger, too. They all served me in their own way.

And so, when I awoke on the first day of January and realized I didn't even *want* to listen to sad songs, I knew something within me had shifted. It's not that I don't feel sadness anymore, because that's just unreasonable, rather that I'm not actively *choosing* to be sad.

That part of the process—the dark night of mourning, the sticky mess of sorting through the mangled pieces of my heart—it was, in some ways, a choice. I *chose* to break myself open in order to heal. I chose to allow sadness to take up residence. I chose not to run from it. I chose to get comfortable with it.

I chose to transmute the sadness into art, spinning tears into gold, doing the alchemy of my soul.

But I also knew that I wasn't going to choose it forever. Time devours everything, and at some point, despite how familiar it had become, I would need to let the sadness go. I could only allow myself to choose it for as long as it served me.

I feel the Phoenix rising now, and I know she cannot rise if I keep choosing sadness as my primary state of being.

And I also feel myself clinging a bit—to Radiohead, to *Weird Fishes*, to the things that kept me tethered to him, to the memory of him, to the memory of us.

These songs were the soundtrack for one of the most profound periods of my life. I needed them then. I don't need them now.

I throw on a William Onyeabor record. It reminds me of a trip to Ojai with my oldest friend, drinking wine from a can, playing backgammon, sharing secrets. I feel my spirit lifted. My feet move to the rhythm of *Body and Soul*.

"If you find yourself in trouble, you better come and dance your troubles away."

I'm smiling as I brew the coffee. I'm choosing something other than sadness. I'm starting to let go.

Gratitude

I always knew I wanted to write books. My 3rd grade teacher, Ms. Aumack, was the first person to encourage me to do so. She handed back a writing assignment with a red penned note in the margin that read, "You're such a talented writer; I hope you write a book someday."

I wrote because I needed to, but I only had the confidence to share what I wrote because of her. I only believed I could do this because someone who was probably younger than I am now saw something in a weird little Hermione-haired girl—something magic, something meant to be shared.

Every time I felt resistance, imposter syndrome, or any other bullshit that tends to come between an artist and their "finished" work, I thought of her.

To everyone over the subsequent 30 years who echoed her words, my gratitude is without boundary. There were so many times when I thought, simultaneously, that I was born to do this and that I couldn't possibly do it at all.

Thank you to the many folks who reminded me I could: My little boo boo head, Jilly and Niffy, Estuy and Glenda, all the boys to whom I wrote poems, all the ones who broke my heart—especially the one who fueled the essays in this book. I am the writer that I am because of the shadows I've been asked to travel.

Lastly, and most importantly, to those of you who started reading my blog back in 2008, and kept reading, no matter what: this only exists because of you. Thank you for giving my words room to breathe, for allowing them to exist outside of my body, and within your atmosphere.

Neghar Fonooni is a word witch, selenophile, Tarot reader, and sometime reluctant healer, born and raised in the City of Angels.

She believes that all art is channeled through the cosmos, messages from the stars that find their way across galaxies, onto our canvases, into the ink of our pens.

She was terrified to publish this book and she did it anyway, because, well, that's just what it's like sometimes. You can book a reading with her and get her newsletter, *Musings for the Moon*, via her website (negharfonooni.com). You can find her other tangible creations at saltandsorcery.shop.

When she's not writing, Neghar is perpetually reminding her teenage son to do his chores, nurturing her 100+ houseplants, lifting weights, and scheming up ways to smash the Patriarchy.

Printed in Great Britain
by Amazon

43712915R00083